HOW TO DRAW!

Fantastical Creatures

Illustrated by
Ted Rechlin

Supplies

- **NUMBER 2 PENCILS**
- **SOFT ERASER**
- **COLORED PENCILS**
- **MARKERS OR CRAYONS**

Helpful Hints

1. Take your time with steps 1 and 2.
Following the first steps carefully will make the final steps easier. The first two steps create a foundation of the figure—much like the frame of a house forms the foundation of the rest of the building. Next comes the fun part: creating the smooth, clean outline drawing of the creature and adding all the finishing touches, details, shading, and color.

2. Always keep your pencil lines light and soft.
This will make your guidelines easier to erase when you no longer need them.

3. Don't be afraid to erase.
It usually takes a lot of drawing and erasing before you will be satisfied with the way your drawing looks.

4. Add details at the end.
Shading and finishing touches should be the last step *after* you have blended and refined all the shapes.

5. Remember: Practice makes perfect.
Don't be discouraged if you don't get the hang of it right away. Just keep drawing, erasing, and redrawing until you do.

 1
 2
 3
 4

Fantastical creatures come from a variety of myths, legends, and folklore. The stories are told and retold throughout the ages and have withstood the test of time. Dragons, monsters, and magical beings—they all inspire our imagination. Now it's your turn to learn to draw these fantastical creatures and add to the legend with your own unique style.

Gnome

The gnome is often described as being extremely small, but with a brilliant mind. He generally has a full white beard and tall, cone-shaped hat. Gnomes rub noses when saying good night to one another.

1 Draw a diamond for the head, and add basic shapes for the body and legs, as shown.

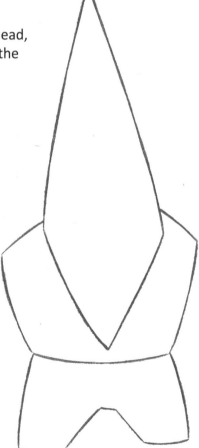

2 In the center of the diamond, draw an area for the face. Add ears, a belt, and feet.

3 Draw in the face and other details. Erase any unwanted guidelines.

4 Add shading and color to your drawing.

Dragon Head

The Dragon Head is said to be a symbol of mysterious power. With spikes around its face and a long forked tongue, its shape is similar to a horse head that is attached to a long, scaly, snake-like neck.

1 Draw a circle and a small egg shape attached to it, as shown. Next, draw the neck.

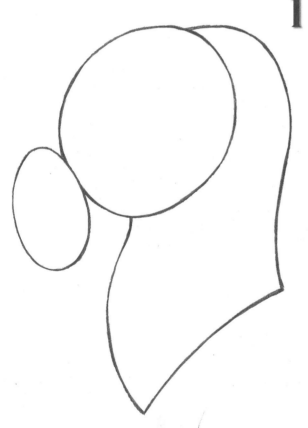

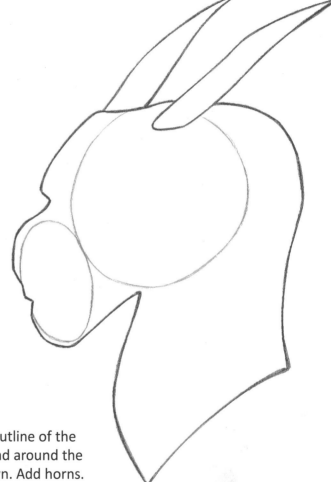

2 Sketch the outline of the dragon's head around the shapes drawn. Add horns.

4 Draw some teeth, spikes, and armor. Add color and shading.

3 Add details, such as the eyes, mouth, and frill. Next, draw the long-forked tongue. Erase any unwanted guidelines.

Chinese Dragon

The Chinese dragon could be described as a very long, scaly creature that walks on four legs. The dragon dance is a highlight of any Chinese festival, representing pride and strength.

2 At the top part of the figure eight, draw a tail. Next, add two oval shapes to the circle for the dragon's snout.

1 Draw a figure eight.

3 Add arms, legs, and details to the face, as shown.

4 Draw flames. Add color and shadowing to give the dragon depth.

Pegasus

A great, white winged horse, Pegasus was sired by the Greek mythological sea god, Poseidon. The magical stallion was born in a far distant place on the edge of the Earth and only a hero with a golden bridle could ride it. Its name means "lightning," creating an image of a swift and graceful flight.

2 Add oval shapes for the head, legs, and body. Connect the head to the body with a partial rectangle.

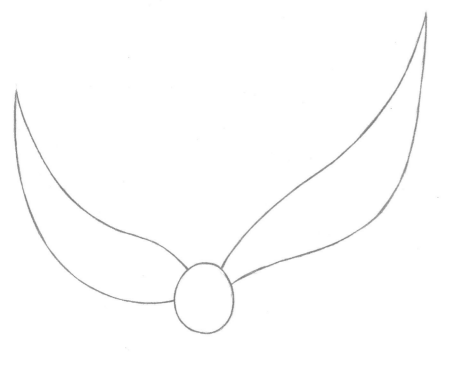

1 Draw a circle and two wings on either sides of it.

4 Add more details, feathers, color, and shading.

3 Add face details and the ears. Next, break the wings into segments, so it will be easier to draw the feathers. Erase any unwanted guidelines.

Mermaid

The mermaid is a fantastical princess of the sea that sprang from the imaginations of lonely fishermen. This enchanting ocean dweller is often described as a beautiful woman from the waist up, with a colorful fish tail where her legs would be.

1 Sketch basic shapes, as shown, for the head and body.

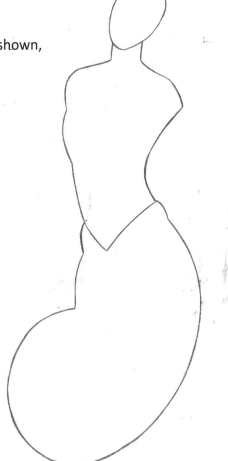

2 Add tube shapes for the arms and the end of a fish tail.

3 Next, add the hair, hands, and a bathing suit top. Erase any unwanted guidelines.

4 Complete by adding final details to the face, fins, and shells.

Gargoyle

The gargoyle is a legend from medieval times that is sculpted out of stone, crouched on a building, with fierce features to ward off evil. When there is trouble, legend states that the gargoyle comes to life as a protector, and battles with its bat-like wings and sharp talons.

1 Draw a large oval for the head, arms, and legs, as shown.

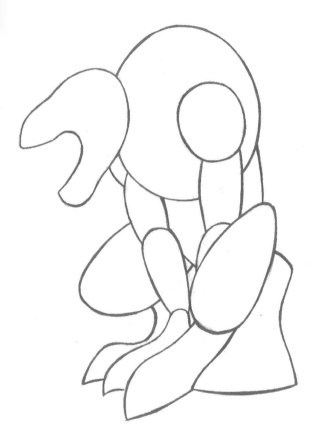

2 Next, lightly sketch in details to the head and arms, as shown.

3 Add the wings, and details to the face and legs. Erase any unwanted guidelines.

4 You are now ready to draw the teeth. Finally, add color and shadowing.

Phoenix

The phoenix is also well known as the firebird. It represents the renewal of the sun, rising from the ashes to restore life. Its giant wingspan stretches across its eagle-like body of golden flames, as its tail blazes light across the sky. Although the phoenix is said to live to be 500 years old, its spirit is reborn and lives forever.

1 Begin with three ovals for its head and body.

2 Draw the wings and the tail behind its body.

4 Fray the edges of the wings and tail for the feathers. Now, add color and shading.

3 Next, draw the beak, eye, and feet. Erase any unwanted guidelines.

Goblin

This green-skinned fantastical creature has very large ears that shoot away from its face. The goblin is usually very angry and crabby, but will find joy causing mischief for others.

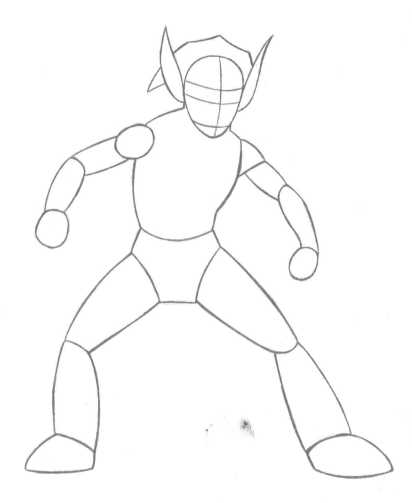

1 Begin with an egg shape for the head and add on basic shapes for the body and legs. Add an area for the loincloth and boots.

2 Add arms, ears, and a hat. Next, add guidelines for the face.

4 Draw a bone necklace. Add color and shading to complete your drawing.

3 Draw the eyes, nose, and mouth. Erase the guidelines, and add bandages and a vest.

Basilisk

A basilisk, known as the king of the serpents, is one of the most feared creatures in all of mythology. It can destroy its enemy simply by looking at it. Its appearance has always been a matter of dispute since there is no way to see a basilisk and survive.

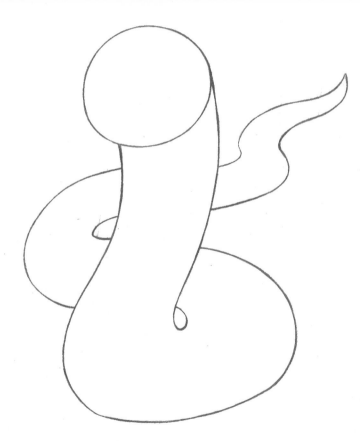

1 Draw a circle for the head and a snake-like figure for the body.

2 Sketch the beak over the head, as shown.

4 Now, it's time to draw the legs to the base and add some teeth and details to the body. Add color and shading to complete this king of the serpents.

3 Add details, such as the eye, tongue, and jaw line.

Campchurch

A campchurch has the fins and the tail of a sea creature, and the body of a unicorn with a horn on its forehead. It is also known as a Sea Unicorn. One of the unique features of this magical ocean dweller is its beautiful mane of hair. A mermaid rides the campchurch the way a person rides a horse.

2 Add the front leg, fin, and some more of the tail.

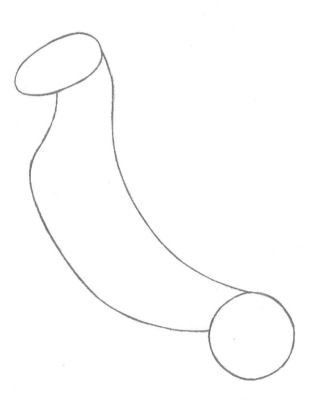

1 Start your drawing with an egg shape for the head, a tube for the body, and a circle for the tail.

4 Add another leg and a flared mane. Finish with more detail, shading, and color.

3 Complete the face, leg, tail, and fin. Erase the guidelines.

Leprechaun

The leprechaun is a funny little fellow from Irish fairytales. He is said to be a quiet creature and a master at making and mending shoes. Legend has it that following a leprechaun to the end of a rainbow can lead to a sparkling pot of gold.

1 Beginning with a circle for the head, draw basic shapes for the body, legs, and feet.

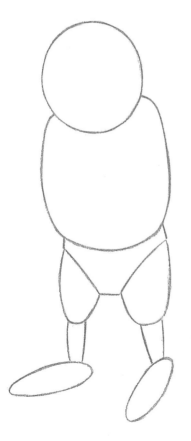

2 Sketch a hat and guidelines for the face. Next, add ears, arms, and hands.

3 Add details to the face, body, legs, and feet. Erase unwanted lines.

4 Finally, add details to the beard and clothing. Draw a cane and a pot of gold. Complete your drawing with color and shading.

Werewolf

The werewolf is considered to be a human that mysteriously turns into a "wolf-man" on the night of a full moon. Werewolves have extraordinary strength, speed, and sense of smell and hearing—far greater than either man or wolf. Its glowing eyes can see in complete darkness.

1 Using ovals and basic shapes, as shown, sketch the head, body, and leg.

2 Next, add the arms, ears, other leg, and feet.

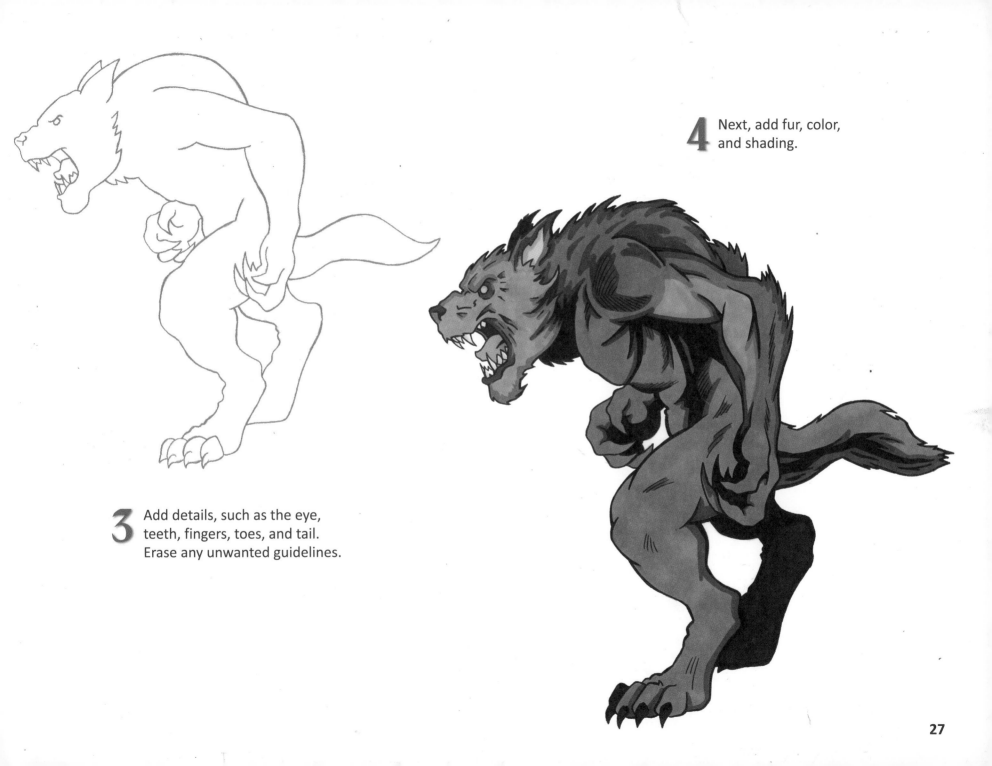

4 Next, add fur, color, and shading.

3 Add details, such as the eye, teeth, fingers, toes, and tail. Erase any unwanted guidelines.

European Dragon

The mythological European dragon is a huge, fire-breathing creature. Resembling a dinosaur, it walks on all fours while dragging its massive tail. Incredibly powerful wings enable this mighty creature to soar through the sky.

1 Draw an oval for the head and attach a curling snake-like body.

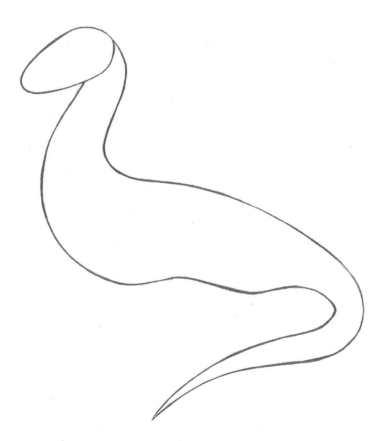

2 Add wings to the back. Next, draw tube shapes for the legs.

4 Now, it's time to draw spikes on the head and back, and scales on the body. Add color and shading.

3 Add details to the face and wings, and draw toes. Erase any unwanted guidelines.

Troll

The troll is a tiny mythological creature that lives in the wilderness. It can make itself invisible, and then reappear at will. Though small, trolls cause mischief to those who stumble into one of their traps.

2 Draw the pointy ears. Next, using tube shapes, add the arms and feet.

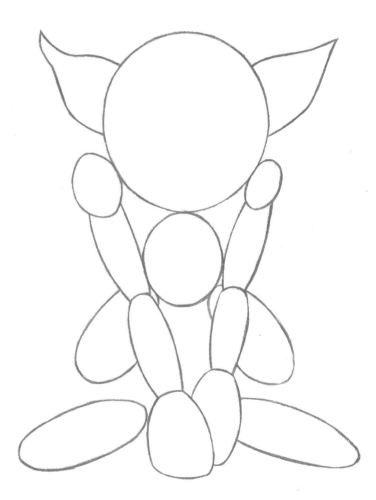

1 Begin with a big circle. Add three smaller oval shapes, as shown.

3 Add the face, and erase any unwanted guidelines.

4 Now, it's time to add details, color, and shadowing.

Elf

The elf is said to be a young magical being that can live forever. Elves can be seen dancing and singing in the forest and meadows where they live.

1 Begin the drawing with an egg shape for the head. Next, add basic shapes for the body.

2 Draw the arms, legs, and hat. Add guidelines to the head for the facial features.

3 Add the details such as the eyes, nose, ears, mouth, and belt. Erase any guidelines.

4 Now, it's time for color and shading. Get this elf ready to hop into the forest!

33

Vampire

The vampire is said to be the most mysterious of all humanoid monsters. This creature of the night has dark lines that surround its features, and white haunting eyes that hypnotize its prey. The vampire's fangs gleam against the moonlight, ready to bite the neck of its next victim.

1 Begin with basic shapes for the head, body, and legs.

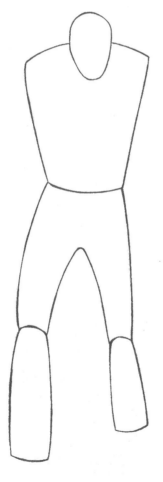

2 Add arms, hands, and feet. Create guidelines on the face.

3 Draw details on the body and face. Add the cape. Erase the guidelines.

4 Enhance the drawing by adding color, shading, and details to the clothing.

Treefolk

Treefolk are the great guardians of the forest. These magical creatures can take on humanoid shapes made up of tree trunks for legs, branches for arms, and tree bark for skin.

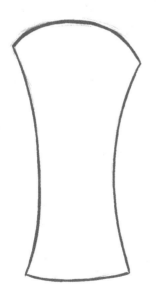

1 Begin by drawing an apple core for the body.

2 Add an oval for the head. Next, draw the arms, hand, and legs.

3 Start to finalize the drawing by adding the face, hair, the other hand, and roots for toes. Add branches to the top of the head.

4 Draw the leaves, branch-like beard, and big shadow on the body. Finish the drawing with color and shading.

Sea Serpent

The sea serpent is a very large sea lion-like creature with a long neck and long tail. There have been over 1,200 reported sightings of the sea monster, though no credible evidence exists.

1 Begin with a large oval for the body. Add a tube for the neck and a circle for the head. Above the oval, add the tail.

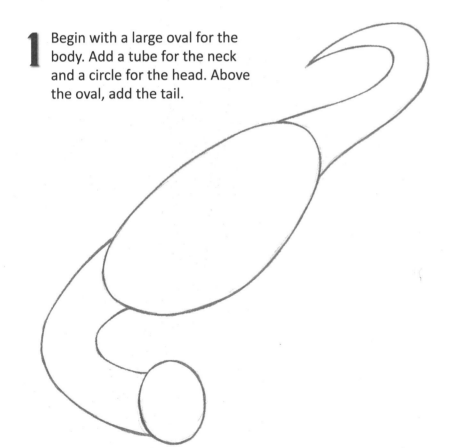

2 Draw two ovals for the snout, and add fins.

4 Add spines to the neck, and draw the teeth and tongue. Lastly, add color and shadowing.

3 Next, sketch in details such as the eye and mouth. Erase unwanted lines.

Centaur

Created by Zeus, king of the Greek mythological gods, the centaur has the body of a horse, which is attached to a muscular man. It has the great speed of a stallion with the intelligence of a human, making it the ultimate warrior. In modern stories, the centaur sometimes has horns, wings, or both. Born from a Greek god and a magical cloud, the Centaur is said to be responsible for great storms.

1 Draw the two shapes, as shown, for the body.

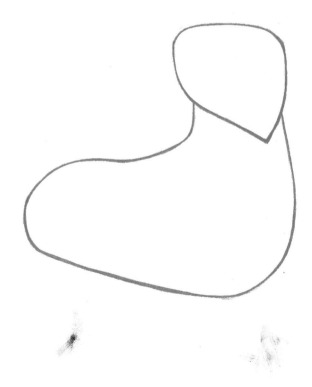

2 Next, add the head. Draw tube shapes for the arms, and add horse legs.

4 Draw in spikes on the armbands, and add a bow and arrow. To complete the drawing, add color and shading.

3 Add details to the head, face, and body. Erase any unwanted guidelines. Then, add the horse's tail.

Zombie

This walking dead ghoul is a shell of its former self. Zombies are mute and have no personality. Some say they have a mysterious infection that causes them to be mindless creatures.

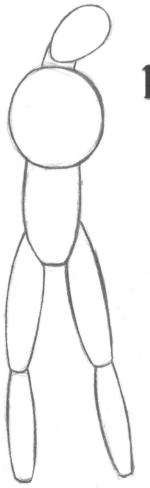

1 As shown, draw these oval and tube shapes for the head, body, and legs.

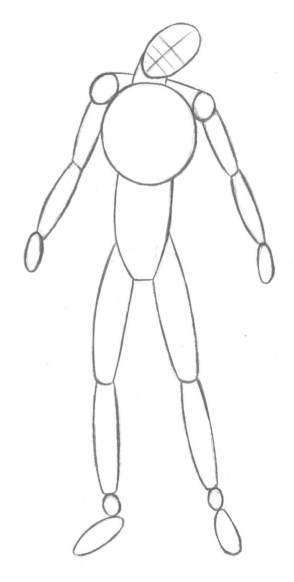

2 Next add arms, hands, and feet. Lightly sketch guidelines for the face.

3 Add details to your figure, such as facial features and clothing. Erase unwanted guidelines.

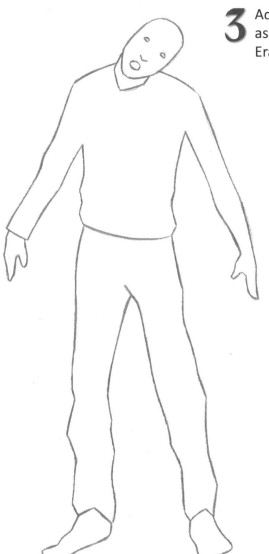

4 Finally, add ragged edges to the clothing, and injuries to the face. Finish the drawing with color and shading.

Wyvern

The wyvern is a type of dragon with two legs and a pair of bat-like wings. Its face looks like a large eagle, and it is able to smash through castle walls with its tail.

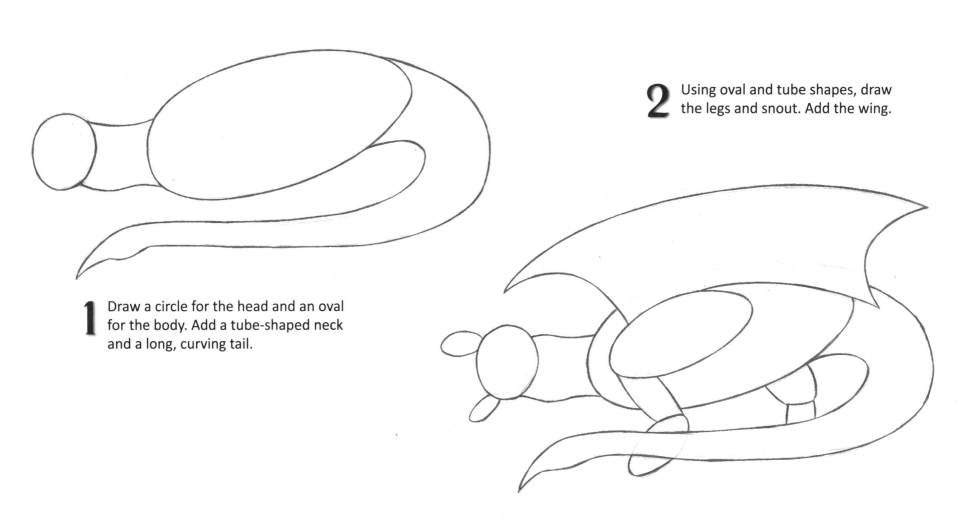

2 Using oval and tube shapes, draw the legs and snout. Add the wing.

1 Draw a circle for the head and an oval for the body. Add a tube-shaped neck and a long, curving tail.

3 Add details to the face, and draw the tongue. Erase unwanted guidelines.

4 Next, add spikes to the head, tail, and face. Finally, add color and shading.

Fairy

A magical being with beautiful, butterfly-esque wings, the fairy is a tiny creature. No larger than an insect, it has the power to grow bigger when it desires. A fairy can be very mischievous and likes to have fun. It is neither an angel nor a human, but some kind of enchanted creature in between.

2 Next, add arms, hands, the other leg, and the frayed end of the skirt. Lightly sketch guidelines for the face.

1 Start the drawing with an egg shape for the head. Then, draw basic shapes for the body and leg, as shown.

3 Draw hair and ears. Add details to the hands and face. Erase unwanted lines.

4 Complete with large butterfly wings, shading, and color.

Ogre

The ogre is a powerful hulking monster with a bald, bumpy, giant head and grotesque, oversized facial features. He is said to be a mean and angry creature that lives in the swamps. A female ogre is known as an ogress.

1 Begin with a large egg shape for the body. Draw two smaller eggs for the legs and a circle for the head.

2 Add egg shapes for arms, hands, legs, and feet.

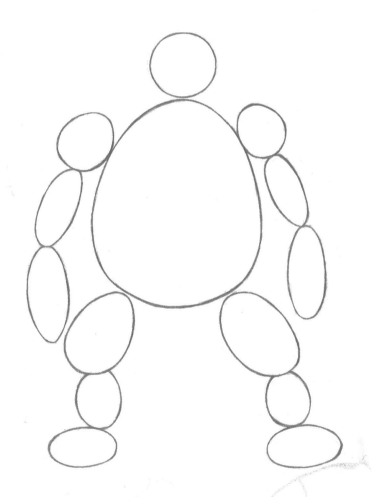

4 Draw in details, such as muscles and the spiked armband. Finally, add color and shading.

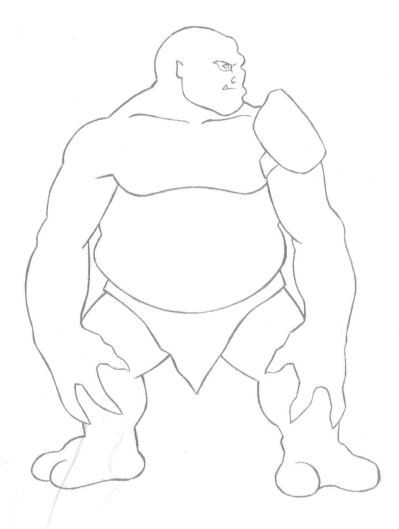

3 Add details to the face, body, legs, feet, arms, and hands. Sketch a loincloth and shield. Erase any unwanted guidelines.

Minotaur

The mythological minotaur has the head of a bull on top of the body of a man. It is so ferociously powerful that it needs to be locked away in a huge and impossible maze with no escape.

2 Add horns to both sides of the head. Then add arms and hands. Draw the split in the hooves on the feet.

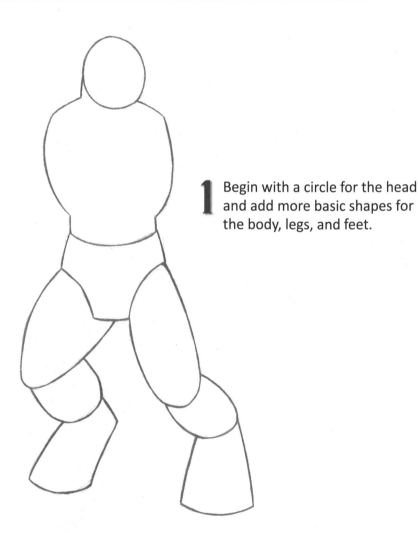

1 Begin with a circle for the head and add more basic shapes for the body, legs, and feet.

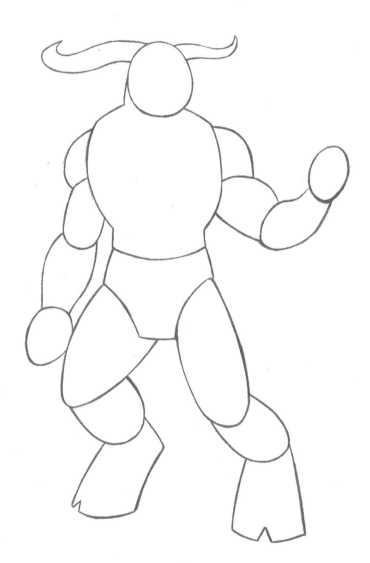

3 Add straps on the arms and a loincloth. Erase any unwanted guidelines.

4 Finalize the drawing by adding the axe, belt details, and armbands. Complete with color and shading.

Kraken

The kraken is the largest mythical monster of the sea. It resembles a gigantic octopus with incredibly long, spiked tentacles that grab unsuspecting ships and drag them down to the bottom of the sea. Legend has it that the kraken plunged from another planet into the Earth's oceans millions of years ago.

2 Add tentacles and arms.

1 Start by sketching four basic shapes, as shown.

4 Complete the drawing with more tentacles, fins, and teeth. Add more detail by adding color and shading.

3 Draw horns and a fish tail. Then, add details to the face and hands. Erase any unwanted guidelines.

Mummy

The mummy is preserved with chemicals and wrapped in strips of white gauze for, what is supposed to be, an eternity. In ancient Egypt, royalty and even their pets were mummified. Great pyramids would be built as their final resting place.

2 Add an egg shape for the skull. Sketch the arms and attach cone-shaped feet.

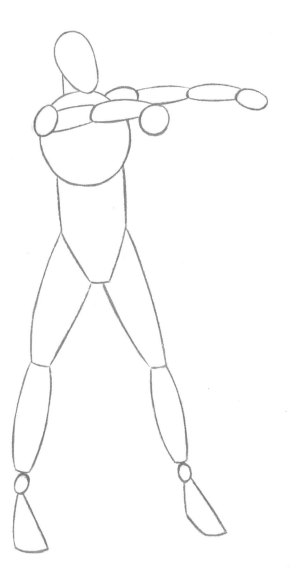

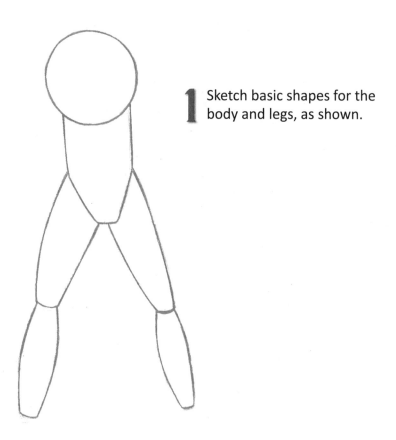

1 Sketch basic shapes for the body and legs, as shown.

4 Complete the drawing by adding lines for the cloth wrap. Then, add color and shading.

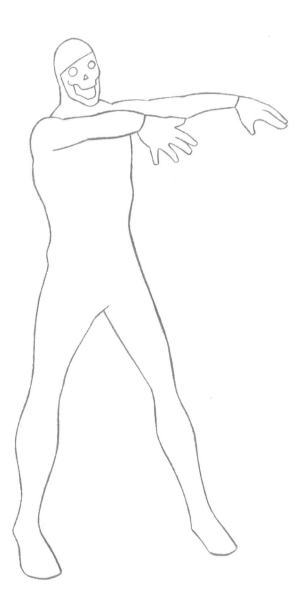

3 Add details to the skull and draw fingers. Erase unwanted guidelines.

Leviathan

The mythological leviathan has a gigantic slithering body, with webbed hands. Its hideous head has ears that look like bat wings, allowing it to glide through the water at several miles per second.

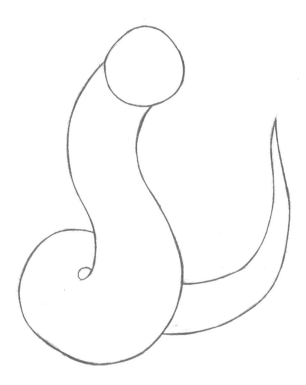

1 Begin with a circle for the head and attach a snake-like shape for the body.

2 Sketch the wings, mouth, horn, and fish tail.

4 Along the body, add black jagged stripes and spikes. Complete the drawing with color and shading.

3 Add teeth, an eye, and a smaller set of wings. Erase any unwanted guidelines.

Bigfoot

Bigfoot, also known as Sasquatch, is the legendary ape-like creature of North America. It is said that Bigfoot is 10-feet tall and has 30-inch footprints. Bigfoot is completely covered in hair, and has an oversized brow and forehead. Experts believe that the dozens of Bigfoot sightings are really those of a bear or ape, rather than of a real creature.

2 Add arms, hands, the other leg and foot, and guidelines for the face.

1 Using basic shapes, draw the head, body, and foot, as shown.

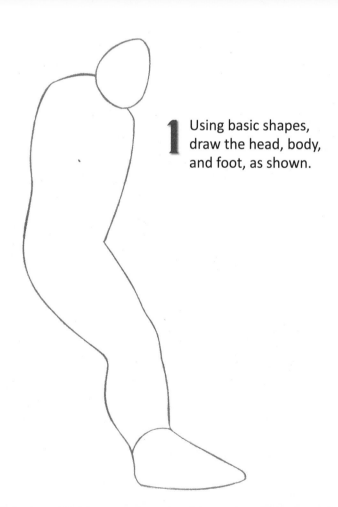

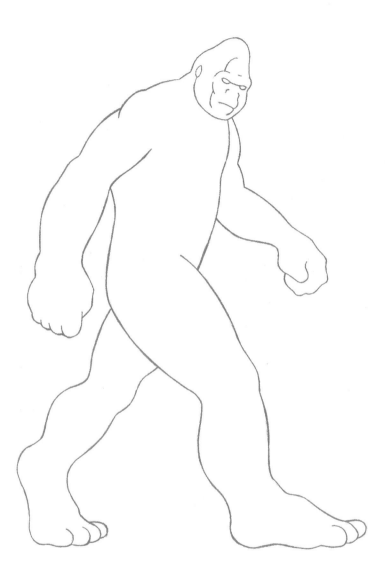

3 Add details to the face, hands, and feet. Erase unnecessary guidelines.

4 Complete this drawing with color and dark shading.

Unicorn

The symbol for joy and light, the unicorn resembles a horse with a horn on its forehead. This glorious animal is often the first creature seen when entering a land of magic and enchantment.

1 Draw a large oval for the body. Attach the neck and head.

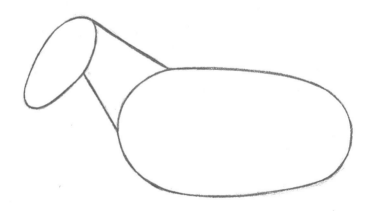

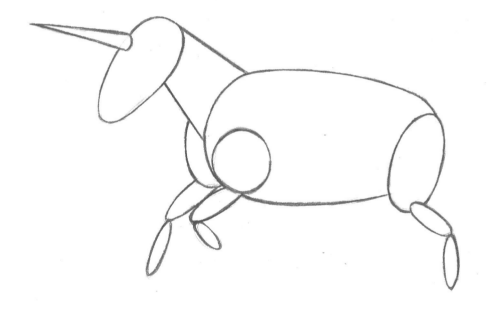

2 Next, add a horn and three legs.

3 Add details to the head and add the fourth leg, which will be a shadow. Sketch in the ears. Erase any unnecessary guidelines.

4 Finally add the mane and tail. Finish off with color, shadows, and shading.

Cyclops

The cyclops comes from a race of mythical giants. It has a single large eye that covers its forehead. Although this creature is feared among mortals, it is a favorite among the Greek mythological gods, because it gave Zeus his thunderbolt and Poseidon his trident.

1 Sketch the head, body, legs, and feet with basic shapes.

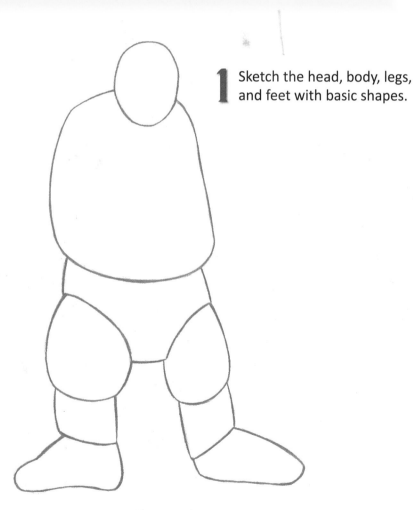

2 Add the eye in the center of the head. Next, sketch the arms and hands.

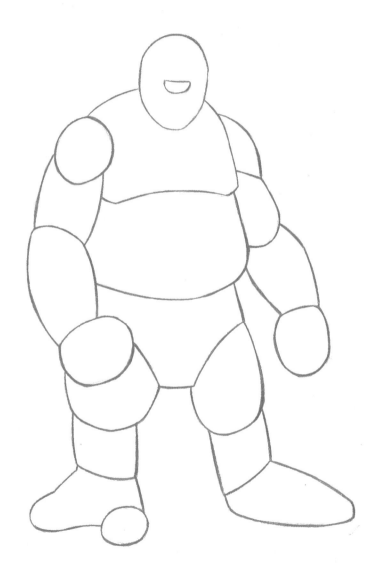

4 Draw in the toenails. Add color and shading to complete the drawing.

3 Complete the face and body with details. Erase unnecessary guidelines.